# Contents

# What's Special about Orchids in Wales?

In Wales, wild orchids are not confined to special sites accessible only by experts; often they grow in quite ordinary places, and they are available for everyone to enjoy. For example, you will see Early-purple, Common Spotted, Heath Spotted, Pyramidal and even Bee Orchids on roadside verges, including some motorway embankments, central reservations and roundabouts; beside village ponds and on cliff-top walks. Even some sheep-grazed hillsides in Wales are home to colonies of Butterfly Orchids.

More than half of the 50 or so wild orchids known to have occurred in Britain and Ireland in recent times can be found in Wales. I use the words 'or so' because part of the attraction of looking for wild orchids is that they do not live by the rules of most flowering plants. One year you might find hundreds of flowers, which then disappear for several years. Just as you are on the brink of despair, fearing that the whole colony has been wiped out, up they spring again, perhaps in even greater numbers than before. Autumn Lady's Tresses is one of several orchids that demonstrate this phenomenon.

Many orchids prefer chalk-rich soil. This makes finding orchids easier in Wales than it is in most other parts of Britain, because with few exceptions our chalk and limestone habitats are to be found near to the seashore. The coastal dune slacks of Wales consist in large part of broken down sea shells that provide a habitat somewhat similar to that of the chalk grassland found in other parts of Britain; consequently, these areas contain many chalk-loving flower species as well as those such as Sea Holly (now quite rare outside Wales) commonly associated with coastal areas. Newcomers to orchid hunting in Wales are therefore advised to start by visiting one of the many sand-dune systems that can be found along the southern and northern coasts. In South Wales there are dunes at the National Nature Reserves at Kenfig and Oxwich and in the north at Ynyslas, Morfa Dyffryn and Morfa Harlech, and at Newborough Warren on Anglesey. Each of these venues is home to at least five and in some cases ten or more orchid species, along with a wealth of other beautiful and fascinating wildflowers.

Dune slacks tend to hold pools of water after prolonged rainfall, and these moist conditions provide the ideal habitat for some of the orchids that are mainly associated with fens and marshes in other parts of Britain. At Kenfig, for example, the rare Fen Orchid flowers in such numbers that the colony found there represents some 50 per cent of Britain's total Fen Orchid population. There, as at Newborough Warren, Marsh Helleborines carpet the ground, and in a good year the displays of Early-purple, Green-winged, Early Marsh and Pyramidal Orchids are nothing less than sensational.

As for timing, with the exception of the Early-purple and Green-winged Orchids, which appear in April and May, and Autumn Lady's Tresses, rarely seen before the start of August, the best time to look for orchids in Wales is during June and early July. In many of the sites mentioned in this book some of the more common species occur in such profusion that it is hard to miss them, provided you are there at the right time.

Not all our native orchids are common, of course, and few are as ostentatious as the exotic tropical hybrids sold as house plants or cut flowers by nurseries and florists today. Some are so downright inconspicuous that they are nigh on impossible to spot even when you are right on top of them; but rarity only adds to the thrill of finding them, and needless to say the ultimate challenge is to find those that are both rare *and* inconspicuous.

There is always the chance of coming across a species that has not been found in a particular place before – like, for example, the sudden appearance of the Burnt Orchid in Glamorgan in 1993 or the more recent appearance in Cornwall of Tongue Orchids that had never before been recorded in Britain. Nobody knows for sure how they arrived, but it is quite possible that Tongue Orchid seeds were carried by the wind. Whether these pilgrims survive there and perhaps spread to South Wales will depend on the effects that global warming has on our local climate. Whether we fry or freeze will decide the future of the Tongue Orchids, Early Spider-orchids and other Mediterranean species for which a narrow coastal strip of southern England is currently the northern limit of their range.

While admittedly many of Wales's native orchids are not as showy as their tropical cousins, there are some notable exceptions. For example, the Bee Orchid and the Marsh Helleborine are, I think, as lovely as any to be found in the world. Sadly, in the past the more beautiful species proved such an attraction to gardeners that many were hunted to the brink of extinction. (In the case of the Lady's Slipper Orchid, Britain's largest native species growing up to 50cm tall, only one plant remained in the wild.)

Today, wildflowers are protected by law, and the best sites where they occur are managed for their conservation. Even so, species are still being pushed towards extinction as a result of intensive agriculture, housing and other forms of development. Now more than ever our native orchids, which are indicators of the health or our natural environment, need our care and protection. The more people who gain a basic understanding and appreciation of these symbolic wildflowers the greater is the chance of conserving for the future those species that we still have.

Lady's Slipper Orchid

# The Nature of Orchids

In many ways an orchid is like any other perennial plant. It needs warmth, light and moisture if it is to thrive, and it needs the help of either animals or the wind to distribute its tiny seeds. But unlike the seeds of most other plants, orchid seeds cannot germinate unless a fungus is present in the soil. Initially, an embryonic orchid is infected by this fungal partner until it overcomes and breaks down the fungal cells to gain nutrients from the soil. The orchid and the fungus live together, but the balance of power between them alters over time. It may be ten years or more before the first orchid leaves appear above the soil surface and a further two or three years before the first flowers appear. Throughout all of this time some orchid species remain dependent on the fungus as their life-support system, whilst other orchids develop the ability to synthesize food all on their own.

Orchids belong to a family known as the Orchidaceae. Within this family are several genera (singular genus) – groupings containing a number of species having key features in common. For example, the genus *Dactylorhiza* includes the Common Spotted-orchid, Heath Spotted-orchid and various Marsh-orchids, while the genus *Epipactis* contains most of the helleborines that are found in Wales. Within a particular species there may be variations of form sufficiently great for botanists to describe two or more sub-species and sometimes within a sub-species a number of varieties.

## Pollination and reproduction

Some orchids - many of the helleborines, for example - are self-pollinating; others are mainly dependent upon insects to carry pollen from one flower to another, and they attract insects in a number of ways. Butterfly-orchids and the Fragrant Orchid produce nectar that attracts insects to them, while the Fly Orchid (a species not recorded in Wales in recent years) secretes imitation pheromones that attract male insects to its flowers.

Bee Orchids look very much like bumblebees resting on flowers, but this visual similarity alone is rarely sufficient to fool real bees into paying them a pollinating visit. (In the UK, at least, it seems that Bee Orchids are nearly always self-pollinated, although there is always the chance of pollination via a visiting bee.)

Given that other orchid species have names such as Man Orchid, Lady Orchid and Monkey Orchid, perhaps we should not place too much significance on names that suggest orchids grow in particular ways in order to attract pollinators!

## Hybrids

Orchids frequently hybridise between closely related types (Common Spotted-orchid and Heath Spotted-orchid, for example) and occasionally between types less closely related. This occurs mainly where two or more species grow close to one another, and the resulting 'hybrid swarms' can make accurate identification of both the pure species and the hybrids very difficult, even for experienced botanists. Sometimes the hybrids closely resemble the parent plants and in other examples they display virtually no similarity to either parent plant. For the beginner struggling to come to terms with the considerable differences in colour and markings within a single species, the presence of hybrids only makes the problem of identification even more challenging. Enjoy the hybrids. Often these plants are taller and more vigorous than pure-bred orchids, and just as beautiful.

# Orchid conservation

In addition to the largely unknown impact that climate change may have on our wildflowers, orchids are threatened by many other pressures. Of these, habitat destruction is surely the most serious. So many hedgerows have been removed, ponds filled in and boggy areas drained that it is a wonder more wild orchid species have not been lost. Intensive agriculture, driven by production-led policy, has resulted in most ancient wildflower meadows being ploughed and re-seeded with high-yield rye grass that requires regular large doses of fertiliser. Frequent spraying with selective herbicides may spare arable crops the need to compete with such wildflowers as corn cockle and corn marigold, but the side effects are not insignificant. Inevitably all these chemical inputs to the soil do not remain where they are applied. Run-off and leaching contaminates much of the surrounding countryside to the point where orchids and many other wildflowers are soon crowded out by more vigorous plants that thrive in a high-input regime.

The recent shift in agricultural policy towards less intensive livestock farming and to organic production of more of our fruit and vegetables is seen by many as a cause for optimism. Certainly there are clear signs of floral recovery on organic farms, and low-density grazing by livestock at appropriate times of the year is a proven way of ensuring that wildflower meadows retain a diverse range of flower species. But unless or until sustainable land-use practices are brought in more widely, the few orchid-rich meadows, woodlands, fens and bogs that have been so carefully protected and managed to retain their biodiversity are not just our environmental crown jewels: they are the seed banks without which any recovery of wildflower richness will be quite impossible. For this reason, if nothing else, it is crucial to retain public commitment, and hence Government investment, to protect and manage the best of our orchid sites, including the national and local nature reserves to which the public has access as well as sites of special scientific interest (SSSIs) some of which are on private land with no general right of access.

The Countryside Council for Wales (CCW) is our national wildlife conservation authority and Government's statutory adviser on sustaining natural beauty, wildlife and the opportunity for outdoor enjoyment in Wales. Part of CCW's remit is to ensure the survival of species and their habitats on Natural Nature Reserves, on SSSIs and, wherever possible, outside these designated areas. To do so requires proper funding. Without the presence of professionals guiding the efforts of the volunteers that they work with on these sites, insufficient monitoring and habitat management work could result in the loss of yet more of our precious orchid species. I raise this matter because a great sadness at the time of writing is that CCW, and indeed Natural England too, are being faced with funding cuts that must threaten the achievements of their conservation objectives. Thank goodness, therefore, that the Wildlife Trust movement is so strong in Wales, for it is largely thanks to their wardens and volunteers, often working with CCW staff, that we still have so many wonderful wild orchid sites.

Another major threat to orchid populations is human predation. Twice in the past year I have set off to photograph rare orchids only to learn that either the flowers had been picked or the plants dug up. Several of our wild orchids are now endangered or in serious decline; they will not survive being moved and replanted in gardens. Take pictures: they *will* last.

# Early-purple Orchid *(Orchis mascula)*

The appearance of Early-purple Orchids in our woodland edges and hedgerows and on grassy roadside verges any time from mid-April onwards means that spring is truly with us - even though the weather might be telling us rather a different tale.

## Identification and habitat

In size the Early-purple Orchid is very variable, typically ranging between 15 and 40cm tall. The oblong basal leaves, shiny and usually dark spotted, form a cluster of between four and eight, with two or three more leaves spread up the stem. The size and number of spots on the leaves also vary greatly from plant to plant. Smaller plants are sometimes mistaken for Green-winged Orchids, although any confusion is easily resolved because of the presence of parallel green veins on the hood of the Green-winged Orchid. The flowers of the Early-purple Orchid, which number between 15 and 50 in a spike, are usually pink to purple although, as seen opposite, there is also an uncommon white variant.

## Where in Wales?

Early-purple Orchids cope with a wide range of habitat types. Widespread throughout Wales, they are a common sight in meadows, on roadside verges and roundabouts, and in coastal sand dunes.

| April | May | June | July | August | September |

# Early-purple Orchid

These white variants were found blooming on a roadside verge in Ceredigion together with a scattered group of Early-purple Orchids with pinkish-purple flowers. White variants rarely occur alone but the unique flower shape immediately identifies them as *Orchis mascula*.

The dark purple spots, absent on white variants, stand out boldly against the pale region towards the throat of these ecclesiastically purple flowers, photographed on the edge of a South Wales hay meadow on a bright late-May afternoon.

# Green-winged Orchid *(Anacamptis morio)*

Although neither as common nor as widespread as the Early-purple Orchid, with which it is often confused, the Green-winged orchid appears soon after the first Early-purple Orchids.

## Identification and habitat

This orchid is one of our most beautiful and is easily identified by the distinct parallel greenish veins on each side of the hood formed by the petals and sepals on the top part of the flower. These veins are never present on the Early-purple Orchid. The Green-winged orchid has up to eight greenish-blue leaves at the base of the plant and one or two more pointed leaves sheathing the stem. The rather loose-flowering spikes each have up to 12 flowers and they often appear in a range of colours within a single colony.

## Where in Wales?

The Green-winged Orchid is found mainly in the dune slacks reserves and is more common in the south of Wales than in the north. Along the Welsh Borders, this springtime species occurs in meadows often in vast numbers.

It is difficult not to spot the green veins, which stand out clearly against the light mauve background of the wings of this exceptionally pale Green-winged Orchid...

# Green-winged Orchid

...whereas a casual observer might at first fail to notice the veins on darker flowered Green-winged Orchids and so misidentify them as Early-purple Orchids.

# Pyramidal Orchid *(Anacamptis pyramidalis)*

Young flower spikes of the Pyramidal Orchid, like the one pictured above, are shaped very much like a (conical!) pyramid; however, when fully mature the common name is rather less apt, because the flower spikes become more cylindrical or sometimes egg-shaped.

## Identification and habitat

At the base of the plant there are up to four green-grey rather narrow leaves and there may be as many as a further six small leaves clasping the stem. The lightly scented flowers, which can number up to 100 in a spike, are various shades of bright pink - the nearer they are to the coast the darker the flowers seem to be. Occasionally specimens with pure white flowers occur, but in Wales they are very rare.

Unlike many wild orchids, whose populations are in decline, the Pyramidal Orchid seems to be extending its range northwards as well as increasing in numbers. The coastal strips and dunes of Wales are the main habitat of these orchids of chalk and limestone, but Pyramidal Orchids can also appear on roadside verges.

## Where in Wales?

The shell-sand dune slacks along the northern and southern coasts of Wales are all good sites for Pyramidal Orchids, which also colonise the drier sides and tops of stable dunes. On the more rugged western coast there are usually a few Pyramidal Orchids to be seen on the cliff tops, but nothing to match the wonderful carpet of pink that they create in dune systems in summers when the conditions are right – warm and sunny but not *too* dry.

# Pyramidal Orchid

Delightfully often, these lovely orchids grow in clustered groups rather than singly.

Pyramidal Orchids keep very good company. Great crowds of Yellow Rattle, Kidney Vetch, Viper's Bugloss and various clovers all share the lime-rich coastal dry grassland habitat in which Pyramidal Orchids are mainly to be found in Wales. (In England this orchid is much more of an inland wildflower, notably associated with chalk downland.)

The only other member of the *Anacamptis* genus found in Wales is the Green-winged Orchid, which favours damp grassland and so the two species are not often seen growing alongside one another.

# Lesser Butterfly-orchid *(Platanthera bifolia)*

Although becoming less common and nothing like as widespread as in the past, it is still possible to find large colonies of Lesser Butterfly-orchids in Wales. Where they occur in numbers the gorgeous perfume of the flowers can be almost overwhelming in its intensity.

## Identification and habitat

The plants of the Lesser Butterfly-orchid and Greater Butterfly-orchid are often much the same size, and so it is very difficult to tell them apart. Both flowers are night-scented, and although we may not be able to tell the scents apart it seems that the insects that pollinate them can, since the two flower species attract different groups of pollinators.

An easy way to distinguish between the two Butterfly orchids is to examine the pollinia - the columnar structures formed by coagulated pollen of the more mature flowers. In the Lesser Butterfly-orchid the pollinia are vertical and parallel to one another, whereas those of the Greater Butterfly-orchid lean inwards towards the top.

These orchids can be found in a number of habitats including meadows and woodland but also on heaths and on marshy ground. The ones photographed opposite were in a meadow in Carmarthenshire, where they grow along with Greater Butterfly-orchids.

## Where in Wales

Widespread throughout Wales, this acid-tolerant orchid is most commonly seen in unimproved meadows; it also grows beside parts of the Pembrokeshire Coast Footpath.

# Lesser Butterfly-orchid

These Lesser Butterfly-orchids together with dozens more provided a splendid summer display at Cae Blaen Dyffryn, a local nature reserve near Lampeter, in Carmarthenshire.

# Greater Butterfly-orchid *(Platanthera chlorantha)*

A few meadows in Wales still have large colonies of Greater Butterfly-orchids and the sight and scent of such large numbers provide a very special experience not easily forgotten.

## Identification and habitat

When growing in the open, the Greater Butterfly-orchid is a sturdy-looking plant usually coming into flower a week or two later than its close relative the Lesser Butterfly-orchid. The cylindrical flower spike, on a stem sometimes more than half a metre tall, can have up to 40 shiny white scented flowers. The scent is strongest at night, when it attracts various hawk-moths and other pollinating insects.

This pallid orchid tends to favour calcareous soils and can be found on chalk grassland and in meadows. Lesser Butterfly-orchids, in contrast, are found in a wider range of habitats than the Greater Butterfly-orchid. Both species are still fairly common in Wales.

## Where in Wales

Greater butterfly-orchids can be seen throughout Wales; they favour alkaline meadows or pasture that is only slightly acidic, but they also occur in some woodland edges. A good place to look for the Greater Butterfly-orchid is Caeau Lletty Cybi, a local nature reserve near Tregaron, in Ceredigion.

# Greater Butterfly-orchid

In Wales no hybrids between the two Butterfly-orchids have been reported, and so the distinctive flower form and the very obvious yellow-brown pollinia at the entrance to the flower spur make definite identification to species level very easy indeed.

# Fragrant Orchid *(Gymnadenia conopsea)*

Not just another 'pink orchid' of which we have so many, the Fragrant Orchid is easily distinguished by its sweet perfume, which at close quarters can be quite intense. Although in decline due to overgrazing, land drainage and the ploughing up of formerly permanent pasture, it is still possible to see good colonies of these orchids in Wales.

As expected of a scented wildflower, pollination is by insects. The Fragrant Orchid attracts moths, butterflies and bumblebees, all of which are effective pollinators of this wildflower.

## Identification and habitat

The Fragrant Orchid, which has an overall slimmer appearance than most of our other wild orchids, can grow to a height of 40cm and have as many as 200 pink flowers packed into a single flower spike. As well as four or five narrow basal leaves, several even narrower leaves grow up the stem.

Experts currently recognise three sub-species of this orchid as native to Britain, and two of them are fairly common locally in Wales; all three may eventually be reclassified as separate species.

## Where in Wales?

Throughout most of the British Isles the Fragrant Orchid is found mainly in chalk- or limestone-rich areas. In Wales it can be found in damp coastal meadows and dune slacks and on the margins of alkaline fens, for example at Cors Bodelio on Anglesey.

# Fragrant Orchid

The fine specimens shown here were photographed at Cors Bodeilio Nature Reserve near Pentraeth, on Anglesey, where Fragrant Orchids grow alongside Narrow-leaved Marsh-orchids and Marsh Helleborines.

# Bee Orchid *(Ophrys apifera)*

Many people's favourite, the Bee Orchid is another good-news story in Wales where it appears to be increasing its range, spreading inland from the narrow coastal dune slacks. Away from the coast, colonies will appear mysteriously in a location one year and then disappear, perhaps recurring several years later but sometimes not reappearing at all.

## Identification and habitat

Bee Orchids can grow up to 50cm tall. Each plant has up to six leaves at the base with a further two stem leaves. The flower, which really does resemble a bumblebee, has three bright pink sepals appearing behind the 'body' of the bee. Plants usually produce between two and seven flowers, but the magnificent specimen opposite had ten.

## Where in Wales?

In Wales Bee orchids are easily found in the coastal sand dune slacks, but they sometimes appear in large numbers along the central reservations of dual carriageways where limestone chippings have been used as a drainage material.

| April | May | June | July | August | September

# Bee Orchid

Kenfig National Nature Reserve was home to this fine specimen, seen in early July.

# Common Twayblade *(Neottia cordata)*

Although common and widespread in Wales, this unimposing orchid is very easy to miss, growing as it so often does in tall grass and in the presence of much showier species such as various Marsh-orchids and Spotted-orchids.

## Identification and habitat

The name twayblade refers to the pair of oval leaves (two blades) near the base of the plant. The flower spike, sometimes up to 75cm tall but usually much shorter in wind-swept dune slacks and sheep-grazed coastal cliffs, can have as many as 100 flowers.

## Where in Wales?

Common Twayblade, which thrives not only on calcareous soils but also in moderately acidic areas, is very common in the dune slacks at Kenfig and Newborough Warren. Its tiny northern relative *Neottia cordata*, the Lesser Twayblade (see the flower inset opposite) rarely grows taller than 10cm, has heart-shaped leaves, and is occasionally found in upland North Wales. Favouring boggy ground beneath heather and bilberry, Lesser Twayblade has, for example, been recorded beside the Roman Steps footpath in the Berwyn Hills. Being small, and retiring in habit, it can be a very difficult orchid to find.

# Common Twayblade

Lesser
Twayblade

The sweet-scented flowers of Common Twayblade attract insects, including ichneumon wasps and beetles, which, in collecting nectar from the lip of the flower, act as pollinators.

# Bird's-nest Orchid *(Neottia nidus-avis)*

Invariably concealed among the leaf litter in dark woodland, the Bird's-nest Orchid is so called because its tangle of short roots resembles a badly made bird's nest.

## Identification and habitat

Lacking chlorophyll, the Bird's-nest Orchid is entirely dependent on another plant or 'host' for its nutrients. The stem of this orchid is thick and the leaves small and bract-like. Each flower spike can have up to 100 densely-packed flowers which are, like the rest of the plant, golden brown turning darker with age. Being tolerant of deep shade, Birds's-nest Orchids are found mainly in broad-leaved deciduous woodland, especially under beech trees where there is a deep layer of leaf-mould.

## Where in Wales?

Given its preference for lime-rich soil and mature beech or yew trees, it's hardly surprising that the Bird's-nest Orchid is rarely found in much of Wales. There are a few productive localised sites in Denbighshire and Pembrokeshire, but our best region by far for this woodland species is Southeast Wales. In the nature reserves of Pwll y Wrach and Cwm Clydach Woodlands, in the Brecon Beacons National Park, Bird's-nest Orchids occur in numbers that vary greatly from year to year.

# Early Marsh-orchid *(Dachtylorhiza incarnata)*

Three sub-species of this gorgeous orchid are common in Wales. The Early Marsh-orchid provides spectacular displays in many coastal dune slacks, often appearing together with two other members of the *Dachtylorhiza* genus, the Northern and Southern Marsh-orchids. Hybridisation with the Northern Marsh-orchid is particularly common, adding to the difficulty of identification of the various members of this complex group.

## Identification and habitat

The Early Marsh-orchid usually grows to between 15 and 30cm tall and has three to six greenish-yellow leaves around the base of the plant and further pointed leaves up the stem. There can be up to 30 flowers on each rather cylindrical spike. The sub-species are distinguished by their very different colour forms and habitat preferences.

## Where in Wales?

Newborough Warren on Anglesey is excellent for Early Marsh-orchids but they can be found in most of the dune habitats throughout Wales including Ynyslas Dunes, near Borth; Oxwich, on the Gower Peninsula; and Kenfig Dunes, near Bridgend. Inland there are also a few scattered fen, bog and damp grassland sites where Early Marsh-orchids have been recorded – generally as minority members of large groups of wetland orchids and hybrid swarms – but the greatest concentrations are all on or near to the coast.

# Early Marsh-orchid

Blushing beauty: *Dactylorhiza incarnata* ssp. *incarnata,* with its stem and bracts more intensely purple towards the top, is a common sight in coastal parts of north and mid Wales. Bumblebees, attracted to the flowers, act as very effective pollinators.

It's easy to be bowled over by the intensity of the red flowers of *Dactylorhiza incarnata* ssp. *coccinea* – especially when you come across several hundred in a single dune slack, which is by no means an unusual occurrence in Wales. (This picture was taken at Newborough Warren, on Anglesey.)

# Frog Orchid *(Dachtylorhiza viridis)*

The Frog Orchid appears to be a somewhat uncharacteristic member of the *Dachtylorhiza* group of orchids. Formerly placed in its own genus, *Coeloglossum*, the Frog Orchid was reclassified following the discovery that its genetic makeup is very similar to that of the Spotted-orchids and Marsh-orchids with which it sometimes hybridises. This orchid is in decline throughout the UK and is now very rarely found in Wales.

## Identification and habitat
Although the Frog Orchid can occasionally grow to 40cm its normal height range is just 5 to 15 cm, making it difficult to spot even on closely grazed turf. There are three to five narrow yellowish-green leaves at the base of the plant and further pointed leaves growing up the stem. The flower spike is compact and the flowers themselves are usually reddish to brown, although specimens with paler green flowers occur in damp shaded areas. The flowers are reputed to resemble frogs: that depends how good you are at visualising frogs!

## Where in Wales?
The Frog Orchid can still be found at Minera Quarry, near Wrexham. Elsewhere in Wales it is found on Anglesey from time to time; and in the past this lime-loving plant was reported from sites in Pembrokeshire, where it is now considered extinct. There may well be other colonies waiting to be discovered, but what makes finding this species so difficult is not only its inconspicuous nature but also the fact that away from its preferred chalk grassland habitat the Frog Orchid's occurrence in any particular year cannot be relied upon.

# Frog Orchid

With more than 25 individual flowers, this example of the Frog Orchid is unusual but certainly not exceptional: specimens with 50 flowers occur occasionally; however, flower spikes with between five and 15 individual flowers are more typical.

# Narrow-leaved Marsh-orchid *(Dachtylorhiza traunsteineroides)*

This orchid is difficult to identify and is often confused with small specimens of other orchids such as the Heath Spotted-orchid, which can tolerate both acid and calcareous habitats.

## Identification and habitat

A more slender and delicate-looking plant than most other Marsh-orchids, the Narrow-leaved Marsh-orchid grows only in calcareous marshes and wet meadows; this can be a help with identification. Above up to three normally unspotted basal leaves there are one or two narrow, pointed stem leaves. The flower-spike has typically between seven and 12 large flowers fairly well separated from each other and ranging from pale pink to dark purple.

## Where in Wales?

Difficult to find as well as to identify, the Narrow-leaved Marsh-orchid has recently been recorded at the Ynyslas Reserve in Ceredigion; it also occurs around the Glaslyn Marshes near Porthmadog, in Pembrokeshire and in Cors Bodeilio, a small area of calcareous fenland on Anglesey.

Left: A Narrow-leaved Marsh-orchid seen growing in the lime-rich fenland of Cors Bodeilio Nature Reserve, near Pentraeth, on Anglesey.

# Common Spotted-orchid *(Dachtylorhiza fuchsii)*

Common this orchid may be, but it is no less beautiful for that. The variations in colour and lip-markings between specimens bear testimony to the diversity that can be found in a single orchid species.

## Identification and habitat

This lovely orchid, which is found throughout Wales, typically grows to between 15 and 50cm but occasionally soars to 70cm in suitably sheltered spots. The leaves near the base of the plant usually carry dark brownish-purple marks, and there are usually four or five more small narrow leaves further up the stem.

The lines and spots on the flowers of the Common Spotted-orchid vary from very pale (almost white) to quite dark pinkish-purple on a lilac, pink or white background. This species is distinguished from the Heath Spotted-orchid by its much deeper incisions in the lip, which is divided into three roughly equal parts. The lip of the Heath Spotted has much shallower incisions and is more rounded, with a much smaller central lobe.

Common Spotted-orchids prefer calcareous soils, and so they thrive in the coastal dune slacks of Wales and in limestone pavement areas such as the Great Orme. These orchids are often to be seen on roadside verges and motorway central reservations where limestone chippings have been used in the construction, and they can appear on waste ground and in meadows wherever the soil is not too acidic.

## Where in Wales?

Abundant and widespread in Wales, the Common Spotted-orchid is found in dune slacks and lime-rich pastures as well as on woodland edges and moderately acidic heaths.

| April | May | June | July | August | September |
|-------|-----|------|------|--------|-----------|

# Common Spotted-orchid

In waterside locations Common Spotted-orchids often occur alongside various marsh-orchids, with which they readily hybridise. The long, parallel-sided spur of the Common Spotted-orchid distinguishes it from Marsh-orchids, which have shorter swollen spurs.

Few wild orchid species vary so much in the colour and boldness of their markings as Common Spotted-orchids. You may find examples that are almost pure white, while others carry reddish-pink patterning on a pale pink background. In the specimen shown above the strident purple markings stand out against a very pale lilac background.

Hybrids between the Common Spotted-orchid and the Fragrant Orchid (page 20) are not uncommon, while hybrids with both the Northern and Southern Marsh-orchid are frequently encountered. The Frog Orchid (page 30) is another species with which the Common Spotted-orchid has been known to hybridise, and this finding has contributed to the argument for the recent reclassifying of the Frog Orchid as a *Dactylorhiza* species.

| April | May | June | July | August | September | *35* |

# Heath Spotted-orchid *(Dachtylorhiza maculata)*

Tolerant of a wide range of habitats, the Heath Spotted-orchid is very common and abundant in Wales. Although the most common pink orchid in upland areas, it will sometimes stray onto the calcareous soils preferred by the Common Spotted-orchid.

## Identification and habitat

The Heath Spotted-orchid seldom grows taller than 20cm and usually has a more rounded flower spike than the Common Spotted-orchid, with which it is frequently confused. The shape of its lower lip is quite different, however, being more rounded and with a much less exaggerated central tooth, with sometimes as few as five individual flowers on a spike and rarely more than 20. The long narrow leaves are lightly spotted and have central keels.

Heath Spotted-orchids show a strong preference for the acid soils associated with heath, peaty bogs and marshland, of which Wales has such an abundance.

## Where in Wales?

It is no exaggeration to say that this species can be found in numerous locations in every county in Wales, and few nature reserves and unimproved hill slopes are without them.

# Heath Spotted-orchid

Heath Spotted-orchids often have rounded flower spikes similar to the specimen above.

# Southern Marsh-orchid *(Dachtylorhiza praetermissa)*

Widespread and very common in South Wales, the Southern Marsh-orchid occurs only in a few locations the north of the country, but then often together with the Northern Marsh-orchid (just to make the challenge of precise identification even more difficult!).

## Identification and habitat

The Southern Marsh-orchid has up to nine unspotted leaves at the base of the plant and several more clasping the stem. Growing to a height of tyically 30 to 50cm and exceptionally 70cm, the flower spike can be very large with more than a hundred flowers that vary in colour from a dusty pale pink to magenta.

At first glance the Southern and Northern Marsh-orchids are very similar, although the magenta flowers of the Northern species are usually much richer in colour than the more subdued Southern species. On inspection, the lip of a Southern Marsh-orchid flower is seen to be more rounded than the distinctly angular lip of the Northern Marsh-orchid.

This robust orchid species produces dense colonies in a range of alkaline or near-neutral grassy habitats. It cannot cope with very high acidity and rarely occurs in dry grassland.

## Where in Wales?

In Wales Southern Marsh-orchids are most common in Pembrokeshire and along the southern coastal strip, where they are particularly abundant in the dune slacks at Kenfig and Oxwich National Nature Reserves. Southern and Northern Marsh-orchids can be seen growing together at Ynyslas, near Borth, and at many other mid-Wales orchid sites.

# Southern Marsh-orchid

Not all Southern Marsh-orchids are slim, as this robust specimen demonstrates. When you come across exceptionally vigorous plants it is quite possible that they are hybrids. Particularly common is the cross between the Southern Marsh-orchid and the Common Spotted-orchid, and the resulting plant is often exceptionally tall with a flower spike comprising 200 or more individual flowers.

| April | May | June | July | August | September |
|-------|-----|------|------|--------|-----------|

# Northern Marsh-orchid *(Dachtylorhiza purpurella)*

Often stumpy but nonetheless beautiful, the Northern Marsh-orchid is often accompanied by a wealth of other lime-loving wildflowers.

## Identification and habitat

The Northern Marsh-orchid can grow to 40 cm, but is most commonly 15 to 30cm tall, and has four to six broad leaves (normally unspotted) that encase the base of the stem. When in full bloom, the quite densely packed flower spike is often flat-topped and cylindrical.

This orchid is often confused with the (usually somewhat taller) Southern Marsh-orchid. A distinguishing feature is the angular lip of the Northern Marsh-orchid, which often appears almost diamond-shaped; in contrast the lip of the Southern Marsh-orchid is more gently rounded. Another way of ensuring that you see and correctly identify the Northern species is to visit a marshy orchid site on Anglesey – Rhosneigr Dunes or Newborough Warren, for example - where the Southern Marsh-orchid does not occur.

## Where in Wales?

In coastal dune slacks and alkaline or near-neutral bogs and marshes in Pembrokeshire, Carmarthensire and Ceredigion the Northern Marsh-orchid grows alongside the Southern Marsh-orchid. Further north into Gwynedd, Anglesey and across the North Wales coastal strip, the Northern Marsh-orchid thrives without its Southern cousin. South Stack Cliffs and the fens on Anglesey are also good sites for this orchid of late spring and early summer.

# Northern Marsh-orchid

Along with many orchids in Wales, Northern Marsh-orchids appear in great numbers in the coastal dune slacks; you will also see it on roadside verges and even in mildly acidic bogs.

| April | May | June | July | August | September |
|-------|-----|------|------|--------|-----------|

# Fen Orchid *(Liparis loeselii)*

Although the Fen Orchid is small and inconspicuous it is a much coveted jewel in Wales's botanical crown: some 60% of the total of Britain's Fen Orchids - a rare species now listed as 'endangered' - occur in two sites in South Wales, the only other known UK location being on permanently wet marshland on the Norfolk Broads.

## Identification and habitat

The Fen Orchid is short and almost impossible to spot when not in flower, because it blends in so perfectly with the diversity of lime-loving plants around it. Like the Twayblades, to which it is closely related, a Fen Orchid plant normally has just two broad leaves, and the flower spike has typically three to six distinctive greenish-yellow flowers.

Along with the majority of other orchid species in Wales, the Fen Orchid lives in dune slacks, and a permanent source of moisture is key to its survival: it requires a water table just below the ground surface. The dune slacks of South Wales satisfy this requirement perfectly, absorbing water during rainfall and maintaining moist sub-surfaces soil for weeks or even months afterwards except in the driest of summers. Should conditions in one dune slack change, the Fen Orchid is able to move on, with its seeds germinating to colonise recently formed slacks nearby where the conditions suit Fen Orchids better.

## Where in Wales?

A careful searcher of the dune slacks at Kenfig, near Bridgend, or at Whiteford Burrows, on the Burry Inlet, should be able to find a number of Fen Orchids. Until the eye has 'tuned in' to them, however, these minute orchids are very hard to distinguish in the grass.

# Fen Orchid

Fen orchids don't rely on insects for cross pollination; they are self fertile and the upward-facing flowers probably gain pollination assistance from the rain.

# Bog Orchid *(Hammarbya paludosa)*

The Bog Orchid is even more difficult to find than the Fen Orchid. It seldom grows more than 12cm tall and can be as small as 3cm. Help is at hand, though – the Rangers at Elan Valley Estate call upon members of the public to come and help with an annual hunt to record the numbers of Bog Orchids appearing there, although this is a species in apparent decline, with fewer plants being found each year.

## Identification and habitat
At the base of the Bog Orchid plant there are two to four small leaves sheathing two swellings called pseudobulbs. from which grows a flower spike with up to 20 tiny flowers (just 2mm across). These orchids usually grow on mats of *Sphagnum* moss where there is a slow but continuous flow of water, but they can also be found on the sides of small streams or in seasonal runnels and flushes of water and prefer acidic soils.

## Where in Wales?
The Bog Orchid still occurs in Wales in a few scattered sites in the central and northern uplands, including the Elan Valley Estate where plants grow in permanently wet flushes on the gentle (but still quite hazardous!) slopes of the upper plateau bog.

# Bog Orchid

Seen here growing among young shoots of Marsh St John's-wort (*Potentilla pallustris*), the tiny Bog Orchids are dwarfed by the rushes, Sundews and Cross-leaved Heath that border the peaty flushes within which these fascinating orchids grow in Wales.

# Small White Orchid *(Pseudorchis albida)*

This orchid is in steep decline throughout the United Kingdom and is now extremely rare in the south, although there are still reasonable numbers to be found in parts of Scotland. In Wales, Small White Orchids are known to exist in just one or two sites. The few specimens that do remain are the subject of close monitoring and protection.

## Identification and habitat

A small and inconspicuous wildflower, the Small White Orchid occurs singly or in small groups, often along with the Fragrant Orchid.

Rarely more than 20cm tall and with up to four broad leaves at the base of the plant and a couple of pointed leaves on its typically 15cm tall stem, this orchid is hard to spot among grasses and other wildflowers. The cylindrical flower spike can have up to 100 closely-packed bell-shaped flowers, each not much more than 3mm across. The flowers fade quickly, those at the bottom of the spike turning brown before the top ones have opened.

The Small White Orchid grows in rough pastures on calcareous to mildly acidic soils.

## Where in Wales

Small colonies have been reported in recent years in a few isolated sites in Mid Wales and North Wales, and because it is so unassuming and easily overlooked it must be a species worth looking out for... just in case.

# Small White Orchid

Above: one of just six plants found in a Breconshire wildflower meadow in 2006. Climate change may be expected to drive the southern limit of this orchid even further north.

# Marsh Helleborine *(Epipactis palustris)*

Perhaps because of its similarity to the familiar tropical orchids sold in nurseries today, many people regard the Marsh Helleborine as the most beautiful of our wild orchids.

## Identification and habitat

Growing to typically 20 to 40cm in height, and exceptionally to 60cm, the Marsh Helleborine has numerous pointed green leaves, the bases of which are sometimes purple. The flower spike is one-sided with usually pink-and-white flowers, although a variant with greenish-white flowers is also quite common throughout Wales.

On a UK basis populations of Marsh Helleborines have declined considerably, but they are present in vast numbers in the coastal dune slacks of Wales where ground-down seashells provide the lime content to the soil which these orchids need. These dune slacks hold pools of water during and after rain and provide moist conditions that suit Marsh Helleborines very well.

## Where in Wales?

In summer the dune slacks of Kenfig, Oxwich, Morfa Dyffryn and Newborough Warren are carpeted with wonderful displays of these orchids, but they also occur in a few inland sites such as Cwm Cadlan, near Aberdare, and Cors Bodeilio, on Anglesey.

# Marsh Helleborine

Although Marsh Helleborines are pollinated by many kinds of insects, including bees, wasps and beetles, vegetative reproduction is probably the major source of new plants.

| | | May | June | July | August | September | *49* |

# Marsh Helleborine

Above: a variety of Marsh Helleborine lacking the reddish-brown pigment also occurs in Wales, and it appears either singly or in small groups within colonies of the more common dusky-pink and white form.

Sometimes referred to a Var. *ochroleuca*, this rather pallid form of Marsh Helleborine is in all other respects a healthy plant, attaining a size and flower count similar to those of the more common red-tinged variety.

In Wales, as elsewhere in the British Isles, there have been no reports of the Marsh Helleborine hybridising with other orchids, although on the mainland of Europe it has been known to form hybrids with the Dark-red Helleborine, *Epipactis atrorubens* (page 54).

# Green-flowered Helleborine *(Epipactis phyllanthes)*

The Green-flowered Helleborine can hardly be described as a pretty flower or even an attractive plant, and its often pendulous flower form suggests an inferiority complex. (In contrast, many of the other Helleborines compare very favourably with the finest tropical orchids and more than rescue the reputation of the *Epipactis* genus.)

## Identification and habitat

The size and form of the Green-flowered Helleborine vary depending on habitat. Out in the open plants can grow up to about 40cm tall with as many as 20 flowers on each flowering spike, whereas in deep woodland these orchids are much darker green over all and considerably smaller, often having just three or four leaves and a short flower spike. The self-pollinating flowers (see picture inset, above) rarely open fully and quite often a plant dies back in autumn without any of the flowers having opened.

Throughout most of the UK the Green-flowered Helleborine is essentially a woodland orchid, mainly growing in chalky beech woods. In Wales, in particular, it is found more often on low hummocks within wet dune-slack systems. The flowers never look as if they are fully open even when this orchid is growing in unshaded dune slack habitats, where the plants tend to be more robust with lighter greenish-yellow leaves.

## Where in Wales?

Nowhere in Wales is the Green-flowered Helleborine common. There are known sites in Merioneth and Flintshire, and in recent years a number of plants have been seen on the sand dune systems of Kenfig, near Bridgend, and Newborough Warren on Anglesey.

# Broad-leaved Helleborine *(Epipactis helleborine)*

Anyone fond of walking in woods and forests is quite likely to come across Broad-leaved Helleborines either in clearings or beside woodland footpaths.

## Identification and habitat

This orchid grows up to 90cm in height and each flower-spike can have as many as a hundred separate flowers. The flowers vary from white-green through pinkish-brown to almost entirely purple with the insides of the cup (known as the hypochile) dark red and sticky in appearance; they can be confused with those of several other generally similar *Epipactis* species. For example a pink-brown or purple-flowered variant could perhaps be mistaken for Dark-red Helleborine, a much rarer find in Wales and more or less confined to a few locations on the limestone pavement of the Great Orme, at Llandudno.

The leaves are distinctive, however. Living up to their name, they are wide and ribbed and quite unlike the leaves of other orchids in this genus. The leaves occur all the way up the stem in a spiral. (Dark-red Helleborine leaves are in rows on opposite sides of the stem.)

Broad-leaved Helleborines grow beside or in broad-leaved and coniferous woodland, and although they will tolerate slightly acid soils they show a preference for calcareous sites.

## Where in Wales?

The Broad-leaved Helleborine can occur in lowland forests and woods just about anywhere in Wales, and has been recorded at altitudes up to 350 metres.

# Broad-leaved Helleborine

Above: This picture was taken in the Broad-leaved Helleborine's classic habitat in Wales, dark coniferous woodland, in this instance at Cenarth, near Cardigan.

# Dark-red Helleborine *(Epipactis atrorubens)*

This lovely orchid is now very rare in Wales, where it grows in rather difficult terrain. Anyone willing and able to undertake the hike will find the rewards well worth the effort.

## Identification and habitat

Growing up to 30cm tall, the Dark-red Helleborine is a magnificent plant with flowers that can be a deep ruby-red, although those more exposed to light tend to be paler with a greenish tinge. The Dark-red Helleborine is sometimes confused with the Broad-leaved Helleborine, especially where, as sometimes happens, the latter has dark flowers; however, the leaves of the Dark-red Helleborine are very different. Rough to the touch and with pronounced veins on both surfaces, they occur in steps upon opposite sides of the stem rather than in the spiral form adopted by those of the Broad-leaved Helleborine.

The Dark-red Helleborine grows exclusively on calcareous soil (unlike the Broad-leaved Helleborine, which sometimes tolerates slightly acid conditions). In Wales this orchid is now confined to the limestone pavement at the Great Orme, at Llandudno.

## Where in Wales?

Anyone wishing to see this plant it is advised to enquire in the Great Orme Centre, where the Rangers are always very helpful. Be prepared for a fairly arduous walk and possibly some scrambling over sharp-edged limestone outcrops!

# Dark-red Helleborine

Above: Springing up from a grike (gap) in limestone pavement, this Dark-red Helleborine has 24 flowers on its spike; exceptional specimens can have nearly twice that number.

# Dune Helleborine *(Epipactis dunensis)*

Patience is required of those hoping to see the Dune Helleborine in full flower. Even when the flower spike is well formed it can be several weeks before the flowers open fully.

## Identification and habitat

Although not generally regarded as a pretty orchid, Dune Helleborine plants are tall - up to 60cm - and imposing, with yellow-green, broad and deeply ribbed leaves that grow in pairs up the stem. Each flower spike has typically 20 lax flowers that are a rather dull greenish-yellow. Like the Broad-leaved Helleborine, the Dune Helleborine blends in very well with its background, especially when in full flower, and so it takes time to spot them.

As the common name suggests, this is an orchid of sand dune systems. Rather than colonizing the damp flat areas between the dunes, this helleborine grows on slightly higher dry ground on the slopes of stable dunes, often in light woodland.

## Where in Wales?

Dune Helleborines can be found in Newborough Forest, Anglesey, where they are at their most plentiful conveniently close to the car park.

# Dune Helleborine

Although Dune Helleborines are known to be self pollinating, there is little doubt that some cross pollination by insects also occurs. Vegetative reproduction, where new flower shoots grow out from the rhizome of an existing plant, is also a possibility.

# Violet Helleborine *(Epipactis purpurata)*

The Violet Helleborine is a 'borderline' inclusion, with only one site known in Wales; however, because it grows almost exclusively in dense woodland habitat it is far more difficult to find than its appearance might suggest.

## Identification and Habitat

The beautiful pink-suffused flower illustrated above is a rare variety (Var. *rosea*) containing no chlorophyll. More commonly the flowers are bright green with pinkish lips – and it is therefore the violet tint of the leaves and stems that gives this orchid its common name.

Growing to typically 40cm but exceptionally to almost a metre tall, the Violet Helleborine's greenish-grey leaves tend to grow in a well-spaced spiral up the stem. The one-sided flower spike can carry more than 50 flowers.

## Where in Wales?

Mainly associated with the south-east of England, this distinctive orchid has been found in Wales only at a single site in Denbighshire. Violet Helleborine also grows in shaded beech woodland at several locations along the England-Wales border, including sites in Gloucestershire, Herefordshire and Shropshire.

# Violet Helleborine

Above: The somber violet suffusion of the leaves and stem is clearly visible in the 'normal' plant (left), but in Var. *rosea* (right) the overall rosy pink colour is just breathtaking.

# Autumn Lady's Tresses *(Spiranthes spiralis)*

This is one of those orchids that can appear in vast numbers one year and then virtually disappear for several years before reappearing sometimes in even greater numbers.

## Identification and habitat

This orchid grows up to about 20cm tall, and its blue-green leaves cling to the stem and look almost like scales. The way in which the flowers grow is the clue to the origin of its Latin name, *Spiranthes spiralis*, since they are in the form of a spiral around the stem, which is densely covered in fine white hairs. Each stem can carry up to 20 (typically 10 to 15) individual flowers, which have a pleasant honey-like scent.

Essentially a coastal species in Wales, Autumn Lady's Tresses can be found on flat cliff tops in close-cropped grassland. This orchid also occurs in considerable numbers on several lawns on the Gower Peninsula and at a number of coastal locations on Anglesey and all along the North Wales coast. Because these orchids are small they can be surprisingly difficult to spot.

## Where in Wales?

Bardsey Island, Ynyslas Nature Reserve in mid-Wales, and the flat-topped cliffs at Sker Point on Kenfig Dunes near Bridgend are three of many sites in Wales where you can see Autumn Lady's Tresses. Timing is critical: the flowers fade very quickly after pollination.

# Autumn Lady's Tresses

Above: Autumn Lady's Tresses often appear in profusion at Sker Point, in South Wales.

# Sword-leaved Helleborine *(Cephalanthera longifolia)*

Although its common name would appear to link it with the other helleborines found in Wales, in fact this lovely woodland orchid belongs to a different genus altogether.

## Identification and Habitat

Growing to a typical height of 40cm, the Sword-leaved Helleborine, also commonly referred to as Narrow-leaved Helleborine, is most often found on woodland edges, rides and clearings and occasionally under roadside hedges. Beneath deciduous trees on alkaline soil, often rich in chalk, is its more usual growing habitat, but it has also been recorded under pines in North Wales.

## Where in Wales?

Another orchid closely identified with chalk-rich parts of southern England, the Sword-leaved Helleborine is also found in western Scotland and a few sites in Ireland, again mainly in the west. In Wales, too, the last outposts – strongholds would be too optimistic a word – of this rare lowland species are on the western fringes of Mid and North Wales.

The Sword-leaved Helleborine has been in decline for a century and more, and in Wales it is now confined to barely a handful of protected sites, having disappeared – temporarily or permanently only time will tell – from many more. For example, a few years ago this orchid used to bloom in Newborough Forest, on Anglesey.

Pollination of their seeds rather than vegetative reproduction is thought to be the main if not only means by which Sword-leaved Helleborines propagate. Typical of woodland edge species, the flowers rely for pollination upon bees that arrive from neighbouring wildflower sites such as hedgerows and meadows. Although producing no nectar, a yellow patch on the lip of the flower attracts the insects – another instance of orchid pollination by deceit!

The Latin name *'longifolia'* means long-leaved, an apt description of the distinctive plant.

# Climate Change – Winners and Losers

If the conditions don't suit it, an animal can move home, often quite quickly. Plant species (but not individual plants) can migrate, too, but that can only happen over many generations, as seeds falling to the north or to the south of their parent plant do marginally better or worse than their neighbours.

The trouble with climate change is that it is no longer a gradual process. Some authorities predict cataclysmic changes in temperature, sea level, rainfall and storminess over a period of just a few decades. What effect is this likely to have on our wild orchid populations?

If the current trend continues and Wales becomes a warmer place, we are likely to lose northern species such as Lesser Twayblade, Small White Orchid and perhaps also Northern Marsh-orchid. But there might also be some interesting inward migrations.

**Early Spider-orchid –**
***Ophrys sphegodes***

With milder winters this Southern European/North African species, currently at its northern limit on the coastal chalk grassland of Dorset, might thrive in the shell-sand dunes of South and West Wales.

**Small-flowered Tongue-orchid – *Serapias parviflora***

First found blooming in the wild on mainland Britain in 1989, this Mediterranean orchid is currently confined to a single site on the Cornish coast. It might well reach South Wales in the near future.

**Greater Tongue-orchid -**
***Serapias Lingua***

The Greater Tongue-orchid has been found growing on a coastal site in south Devon and may well have been the result of wind-borne seed. Time, and the increasing impact of climate change, will tell…

There are many other potential gains and losses as a result of climate change, but like other man-made influences on the natural environment the net result (if history is any guide) is unlikely to be an increase in biodiversity. On the precautionary principle, therefore, efforts to reduce our environmental impact are unlikely to be wasted… unless, as some pessimists (who would most probably call themselves realists) are now suggesting, it is already too late.

# Where to see Wild Orchids in Wales

Our wild orchids grow in many places and in diverse habitats. Some pop up in what seem to be the most unlikely spots - motorway reservations, front gardens, and waste and spoil tips to name but a few. Some of these become established sites where the plants regularly recur, while in other places orchids make only occasional appearances.

Many of the rarer orchids live in areas well known for their floral diversity; these are often nature reserves or designated sites of special scientific interest. The Elan Valley Estate is a good example, containing as it does broadleaf woodland and conifer plantations; meadows and heathland; boggy moorland, rivers and reservoirs. Some rare species occur on private land or other places where there is restricted access. If in doubt about public access, please enquire before going on to land that does not have clearly signed access points. And please encourage everyone to treat wild orchids with respect. Even species occurring in large numbers at one site may be extremely rare elsewhere, and all wildflowers are under pressure from climate change, intensive agriculture, industrial and housing development… and even human predation. Wild orchids invariably die when transplanted (whether illegally or with the landowner's consent) to places where they do not normally occur; it is therefore really important to love them and then leave them.

Here is a small selection of locations of various habitat types where, provided you visit at the right time of year, you can be pretty sure of seeing many of our more common orchids:

## Sand dunes and dune slacks

Kenfig Nature Reserve, near Bridgend; Oxwich Bay, on the south of Gower Peninsula; Pembrey Burrows, near Kidwelly; Whiteford Burrows, near Llanmadoc north Gower); Ynyslas Sand Dunes, near Borth; Morfa Harlech and Morfa Dyffryn, between Harlech and Barmouth; Newborough Warren and Newborough Forest (Dune Helleborine) on Anglesey.

**Species**: Early-purple, Early Marsh, Southern Marsh (but not at Newborough Warren), Northern Marsh, Pyramidal, Green-winged, Fragrant (especially Kenfig), Common Spotted, Bee, Marsh and Green-flowered Helleborines, Fen Orchid (at Kenfig and Whiteford Burrows), Common Twayblade.

## Moorland bogs, marshes and lake margins

Dowrog Common, in Pembrokeshire; Pennar Fawr, at Plwmp near Cardigan; Cors Caron, near Tregaron; Cors Fochno, near Borth; Llangorse Lake, near Bwlch, in Brecon Beacons National Park; Kenfig Pool, near Bridgend; Lake Vyrnwy, near Welshpool; Cwm Idwal National Nature Reserve, in Snowdonia.

**Species**: Heath Spotted, various Marsh-orchids. Also Bog Orchid (Elan Valley).

## Fenland

Cors Bodeilio on Anglesey; Corsydd Llyn (four fens, of which Cors Geirch is the largest, on the Lleyn Peninsula); Cors Goch, Near Trawsfynydd; Crymlyn Bog, near Swansea.

**Species**: various Marsh-orchids including the rare Narrow-leaved Marsh-orchid, Heath Spotted, Common Spotted, Early-purple, Fragrant, Greater Butterfly, Marsh Helleborines.

# Cliff tops

Sker Point near Bridgend; South Gower Cliffs; Pembrokeshire Coast Path; Cwmtudu Cliffs, Ceredigion; South Stack Cliffs, near Holyhead, and Cemlyn, near Cemaes (Anglesey); Great Orme, at Llandudno.

**Species**: Autumn Lady's Tresses, Heath Spotted, Common Spotted, Pyramidal, Common Twayblade; also Dark-red Helleborine (Great Orme).

# Lowland Heath

Across much of Pembrokeshire, including Dowrog Common, near St Davids, and the Preseli Hills, lowland heath is the dominant habitat. There are also good sites on the Gower Peninsula; in the Brecon Beacons; in Snowdonia, including the Lleyn Peninsula; and at Penrhoslligwy, on the eastern side of Anglesey.

**Species**: Heath Spotted, Common Spotted, various Marsh-orchids.

# Meadows

Pentwyn Farm Reserve, near Monmouth; Vicarage Meadows and Cae Pwll y Bo, near Abergwesyn; Elan Valley Estate, Rhayader; Dyfnant Meadows, near Llangadfan; Caeau Tan y Bwlch, on the Lleyn Peninsula; Cae Blaen Dyffryn, near Lampeter; Caeau Llety Gybi, near Tregaron.

**Species**: Greater Butterfly, Lesser Butterfly, Heath Spotted, Common Spotted, Early-purple, Green-winged, Fragrant, Small White (extremely rare), Frog, Common Twayblade.

# Woodland

Allt Rhyd y Groes, between Lampeter and Rhandirmwyn; Nicholaston Woods, near Oxwich; Cwm Clydach Woodlands, west of Abergavenny; Springdale Farm, between Usk and Llantrisant; Elan Valley Estate, near Rhayader; Pwll y Wrach, in Brecon Beacons National Park; Newborough Forest, on Anglesey; Cenarth Woods, near Cardigan.

**Species**: Green-flowered and Broad-leaved Helleborine, Bird's-nest Orchid (mature Beech woods are best), Early-purple, Common Twayblade, Common Spotted. Sword-leaved Helleborine and Violet Helleborine also favour woodland edges and clearings, and so it's always worth keeping an eye open for these special rarities... just in case.

# Who Cares for the Wild Orchids in Wales?

The Countryside Council for Wales (www.ccw.gov.uk) is the national conservation authority and advisor on sustaining the natural beauty and wildlife of Wales and on increasing the opportunities for enjoyment of the countryside. On its own, this relatively small organization could achieve very little, and so its staff work in partnership with many other public, private and voluntary bodies to restore and protect natural habitats. Everyone who loves wildflowers and visits orchid sites in Wales benefits from this work, and I for one am grateful to all those through whose efforts we can enjoy today's floral diversity and abundance. Upon their skill and dedication rest our hopes for tomorrow's biodiversity.

The Wildlife Trust movement (www.wildlifetrust.org) is particularly active in Wales, managing dozens of sites and reserves including many containing wild orchids. For example, North Wales Wildlife Trust works with Plantlife (www.plantlife.org) and other partners to manage a reserve at Caeau Tan y Bwlch, on the Lleyn Peninsula, where visitors can see several orchid species and many other rare and lovely wildflowers. As a Wildlife Trust volunteer I have been able to make a small contribution to the work, and as a member I can still continue to contribute towards the resources so crucial to this cause.

The National Trust (www.nationaltrust.org.uk) owns more than 100,000 acres of countryside in Wales, including many sites of wildflower interest. The RSPB (www.rspb.org.uk) has twelve reserves in Wales, all of which are managed to protect wildflowers as well as birds and other wildlife. For example Carngafallt, near Rhayader, in Powys, includes some of the finest moorland in Wales. Pembrokeshire, Brecon Beacons and Snowdonia National Parks (www.cnp.org.uk) also include large areas of orchid-rich moorland and heath with public footpath access. Local Authorities, the Woodland Trust, the Forestry Commission and many others are also involved in orchid conservation.

**The author with hybrid orchids and other wildflowers on a South Wales roadside**

# Acknowledgements

While recognising the crucial role of so many in conserving wild orchids in Wales, I must also say a special thank you to some of the people who helped me during the writing of this book. Thanks, then, to Andy Jones of CCW for advice on identifying 'difficult' species and hybrids; to Rob Petley-Jones for allowing me to use his lovely photographs of Dark-red Helleborine; to Pete Jennings, who helped in my search for the elusive Bog Orchid on the Elan Valley Estate; Wil Sandison of CCW for help in finding Dune Helleborines; and Sally Pidcock for help in locating the Dark-red Helleborine on The Great Orme. Thanks also to Helen Johnston, of Pembrokeshire Rivers Trust; Graham Holmes, of Kenfig National Nature Reserve; and finally Pat O'Reilly, my partner in life and flowers, for his steadfast faith in the project, editing skills and company on the many thousands of miles we travelled to get the photographs